MAN UP

FINAL EVALUATION REPORT

manup.org.au

ISBN: 978-0-646-98539-8

Suggested citation: Lockley A, King K, Schlichthorst M, Phelps A, Pirkis J. (2018). *Man Up*: Final Evaluation Report. University of Melbourne: Melbourne

apo
stro
phe.
press

www.apostrophe.press

TABLE OF CONTENTS

EXECUTIVE SUMMARY

Man Up is a 3 part documentary that explores the relationship between masculinity and suicide. *Man Up* takes Sydney radio personality, Gus Worland, on a journey where he talks with men who have experienced suicidal crises, explores a range of suicide prevention initiatives designed to encourage men to open up to their mates, and creates a campaign ad to raise awareness about the damage caused by men not reaching out for help. *Man Up* was screened by the Australian Broadcasting Corporation (ABC) in primetime over three consecutive weeks in October and November 2016. The documentary was accompanied by a comprehensive digital strategy comprising a website and a social media campaign.

Man Up came about through a collaboration between the Movember Foundation, the University of Melbourne and Heiress Films. Our team was motivated to create *Man Up* by the fact that over 2,000 men and boys take their own lives in Australia each year. We hypothesised that there might be something about *being male* that might explain why males are at far greater risk of dying this way than females. We postulated that masculine norms – that is, the internalised perceptions of what is acceptable and expected male behaviour that guides how men act – might exert an influence. This got us thinking that a large-scale intervention that challenges these norms and encourages men to lower their guard and reach out to others when times are tough might help. We realised that for such an intervention to be successful, it would need to speak to men in a way that is empowering and contains messages that redefine help-seeking as being about taking control of the situation rather than a sign of weakness. *Man Up* seemed to be an ideal solution.

We conducted a multi-faceted evaluation of *Man Up*. We ran a randomised controlled trial (RCT) that gauged how efficacious the documentary was in bringing about changes in help-seeking intentions and views of masculinity in a controlled environment. We posted a survey online to examine similar outcomes in the real world. We also conducted analyses of website and social media data to examine the collective impact of the documentary and broader digital campaign. We drew on combinations of these elements in two final evaluation exercises that considered whether *Man Up* had changed the way men viewed the term "man up" and which specific segments of *Man Up* resonated with audiences.

Our RCT showed that *Man Up* was efficacious in terms of increasing men's likelihood of seeking help in tough times and encouraging their friends to do the same, and shifting their views of masculinity. Our online survey suggested that it was effective in enabling men to recognise societal pressures to repress their emotions and be stoic, and increasing their desires for closer relationships with their male friends. These impacts were further underscored by the wealth of positive emails and social media posts about changes in men's attitudes and behaviours. These outcomes are positive and are made all the more so by the fact that the documentary, and the digital campaign that surrounded it, had such a broad reach.

Our evaluation suggests that the visibility of *Man Up* itself should be maintained and built upon. Opportunities for screening *Man Up* in different contexts and for different audiences should be explored, both within Australia and overseas. Broadening the reach of *Man Up's* messages has the potential to save the lives of men around the world by shining a spotlight on the relationship between masculinity and suicide.

1. ABOUT MAN UP

Man Up is a 3 part documentary that explores the relationship between masculinity and suicide. The documentary title, *Man Up,* deliberately challenges the conventional use of the phrase which encourages men and boys to suppress negative emotions and try to deal with problems on their own. *Man Up* is hosted by Sydney radio personality Gus Worland, one of "the manliest men on radio". In Episode 1, Gus talks with men who have experienced suicidal crises about what led them to that point, and what got them through. In Episode 2, he explores a range of suicide prevention initiatives being implemented by organisations and individuals to encourage men to open up to their mates. In Episode 3, Gus creates a campaign ad with the tag-line *Man Up, Speak Up* to raise awareness about the damage caused by men not reaching out for help. Gus is key to getting the message out to the target audience because men identify with him. He is also personally invested in the cause, having lost a close friend and mentor to suicide.

Man Up was screened by the Australian Broadcasting Corporation (ABC) in primetime over three consecutive weeks in October and November 2016. It garnered an average viewership of 642,000 for each of its three episodes on that initial screening. These numbers have continued to increase because it has been rescreened twice to date and remains available on the ABC's catch-up service, iView.

The documentary release was accompanied by a comprehensive digital strategy comprising a website and a social media campaign. The *Man Up* website (www.manup.org.au) was launched two months before the documentary went to air for the first time (August 2016). It promoted the October release and provided additional information and resources ranging from statistics and research about suicide, to personal stories, and information about different support programs around Australia. It also encouraged help-seeking, providing links to and descriptions of a range of service providers. The website remains live today and continues to allow for ongoing viewing of the documentary (see Box 1).

Box 1: The *Man Up* website home page, with links to each of the three episodes

ONE BLOKE'S MISSION TO SAVE AUSSIE MEN

HOME • TV SERIES • BLOKELORE • MAN·UP • THE FACTS • TV BLOG • HELP A MATE

EPISODES

EPISODE 1
Suicide is the #1 killer of Aussie men under 45. Triple M's Gus Worland is on a mission to find out why.

WATCH NOW

EPISODE 2
Gus travels Australia in search of solutions and discovers some organisations that give him hope.

WATCH NOW

EPISODE 3
Gus creates a campaign to show suicide is not a solution. And he's singing his message for all to hear.

WATCH NOW

Box 2: The *Man Up* social media campaign

Social Media Campaign															
Month	August			September				October				November			
Week Number	1	2	3	4	5	6	7	8	9	10	11	12	13	14	
Show Free-to-Air Broadcast										!	!	!			
Promotion Phase 1				WATCH THE SHOW											
Promotion Phase 2							TALK AND SHARE								
Promotion Phase 3										TAKE ACTION					

The social media campaign also began in August 2016 and ran for 14 weeks, straddling screening period of the show. The campaign was run in three phases (see Box 2) across five platforms (Twitter, Facebook, Instagram, YouTube and Tumblr), and was designed to amplify *Man Up*'s messaging and reach the widest possible audience. Phase 1 promoted the show, Phase 2 encouraged people to share content and discuss issues, and Phase 3 prompted them to take action.

2. THE TEAM BEHIND *MAN UP*

Man Up was the result of a collaboration between the Movember Foundation, the University of Melbourne and Heiress Films. The Movember Foundation funded *Man Up* and was and has continued to be actively involved in promoting it. The University of Melbourne advised on its content and evaluated its impact. Heiress Films made the documentary and created and curated the website and social media campaign.

3. THE CATALYST FOR *MAN UP*

Our team was motivated to create *Man Up* by the high rates of suicide among males in Australia. In 2016, 2,151 males took their own lives, including over 100 who were aged less than 20.[1] This equates to a rate of 17.9 per 100,000 (see Figure 1).[1]

A stark way to visualise this is to think of the Melbourne Cricket Ground full to capacity with men and boys for the Boxing Day Test. By the end of the following year, 18 of those males will have died by their own hand.

Figure 1: Suicide rates per 100,000 per year, Australia

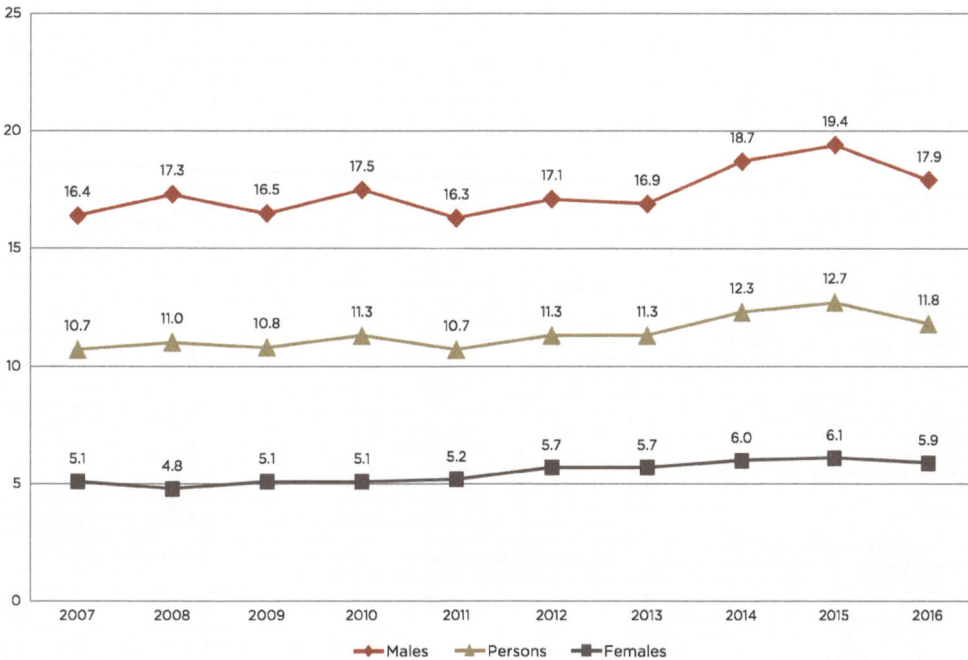

Importantly, male suicides account for three quarters of all suicides.[1] These striking statistics led us to wonder whether there was something about *being male* that might put men and boys at heightened risk. We postulated that masculine norms – that is, the internalised perceptions of what is acceptable and expected male behaviour that guides how men act – might exert an influence. We looked at data from 13,884 men participating in *Ten to Men, the Australian Longitudinal Study on Male Health*. Our analysis showed that, after controlling for other key predictors, one characteristic of dominant masculinity – self-reliance – stood out as a risk factor for suicidal thinking.[2] Other research has consistently shown that conformity to masculine norms is associated with reduced help-seeking and a range of negative psychological outcomes including poor mental health, substance use and suicidality,[3-7] and may contribute to men trying to solve problems on their own rather than reaching out to others.[8,9]

We began to think that to lower the male suicide rate, and improve men's mental health more generally, might require a large-scale intervention that leads them to challenge potentially harmful masculine norms and promote help-seeking to them in a way that resonates with them.[10] We realised that for such an intervention to be successful, it would need to speak to men in a way that is empowering and contains messages that redefine help-seeking as being about taking control of the situation rather than a sign of weakness.[10-12]

Man Up seemed to be an ideal solution. We thought that if we could create a documentary and collateral materials that addressed these issues, we might be onto a winner. *Man Up*'s central themes therefore included that there is no shame in reaching out to others for help, and that mates should check in with each other, especially when times are tough.

4. EVALUATING *MAN UP*

This relationship between conformity to certain masculine norms and reluctance for men to reach out when they experience stress, depression or suicidal thoughts was at the heart of our evaluation strategy for *Man Up*.

Our evaluation was multi-faceted, and each element contained quantitative and qualitative components. We conducted a randomised controlled trial (RCT) to gauge how efficacious the *Man Up* documentary was in bringing about a change in help-seeking intentions in a controlled situation.[13,14] We posted a survey online to examine similar outcomes in the real world.[15] In both cases, we included a focus on the extent to which *Man Up* prompted men to think about their conformity to masculine norms.[13-15] We also conducted analyses of website and social media data to examine the collective impact of the documentary and broader digital campaign.[16-19] We drew on combinations of these elements in two final evaluation exercises that considered whether *Man Up* had changed the way men viewed the term "man up"[13] and which specific segments of *Man Up* resonated with audiences.[20]

THE RANDOMISED CONTROLLED TRIAL

RCTs are commonly used to assess the efficacy of new drugs or other forms of therapy, and they are regarded as the scientific "gold standard". Participants in RCTs are randomly allocated to a group that receives the given intervention or a group that receives some sort of placebo or "control". Baseline information is collected from participants in both groups before they take part, and follow-up information is collected once they have been exposed to the intervention or control condition; this allows changes in a particular outcome to be assessed. The hypothesis usually is that changes will be observed in the intervention group but not the control group. The randomisation process is important because it irons out potential between-group biases and creates a level playing field, which means that if changes are seen in the outcome, then a reasonable explanation is that they were caused by the intervention.

To our knowledge, our use of the RCT design to test the impact of a documentary is a world first. We recruited men aged 18 or more and randomly allocated them to a group that viewed *Man Up* (the intervention group) or group that viewed a documentary that was similar in format but had unrelated content called *Test Your Brain* (the control group). Ultimately, we had data from

169 intervention group participants and 168 control group participants.

Participants attended a group meeting with our researchers where they were enrolled in the trial and completed a baseline questionnaire. The baseline questionnaire incorporated various validated instruments like the General Help Seeking Questionnaire[21] and the Conformity to Masculine Norms Inventory[10] and allowed us to gauge how our participants scored on our outcomes of interest before they viewed *Man Up* or *Test Your Brain*. Once they had completed the baseline questionnaire, participants went away and watched their allocated documentary online at some point in the following week, and answered some questions about their immediate responses to it. Four weeks later, participants completed a follow-up questionnaire which contained questions from both of the previous questionnaires, plus some additional open- and closed-ended questions about changes they may have observed in their own attitudes and behaviours that they attributed to watching the documentary. Participants completed all three questionnaires online.

THE RESULTS

The 169 men who watched *Man Up* had an immediate positive reaction to it. The vast majority enjoyed it, thought it would have a positive impact on men's health and well-being, and indicated that they would recommend it to their friends and family (see Table 1).

Table 1: Immediate responses to *Man Up*

Question	
Did you enjoy watching the documentary?	Mean rating
(0 = not at all, 10 = very much)	8.27
Do you think that the documentary will have a positive impact on men's health and wellbeing?	Mean rating
(0 = not at all, 10 = will have a large impact)	7.92
Would you recommend watching the documentary to your friends or family?	Freq (%) responding "Yes"
(Yes/No)	160 (94.7)

The men who viewed *Man Up* demonstrated some significant changes from baseline to follow-up. After viewing the documentary, they indicated that they were more likely to seek help if they were facing difficulties (see Figure 2). They were also significantly more likely to recommend that a male friend seek help if he was experiencing difficulties and to do the same for a female friend (see Figures 3 and 4).

They also demonstrated a shift in their conformity to traditional masculine norms (see Figure 5). Men who viewed *Test Your Brain* did not show any significant changes against these core outcome measures, leading us to conclude that *Man Up* was responsible for these changes.

Figure 2: Change in help-seeking intentions – self*

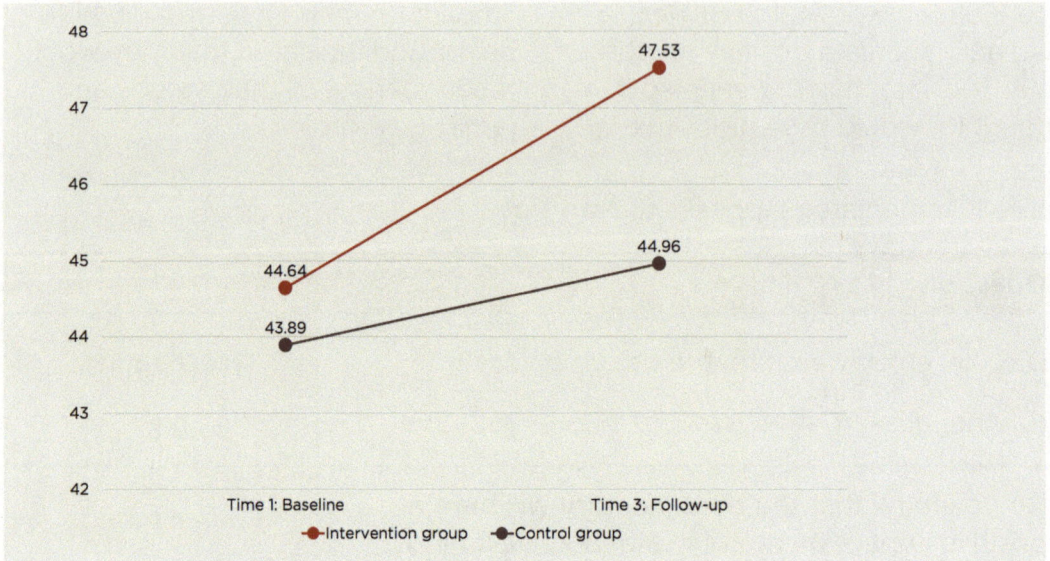

*Response to 10 General Help Seeking Questionnaire (GHSQ) questions
"If you were having a personal or emotional problem, how likely is it that you would
seek help from the following people or services (e.g., intimate partner, friend,
doctor)?" 10 questions each scored from 1 (extremely unlikely) to 7 (extremely likely).
Total score used for analysis; means for each group reported here.

Figure 3: Change in help-seeking intentions – male friend*

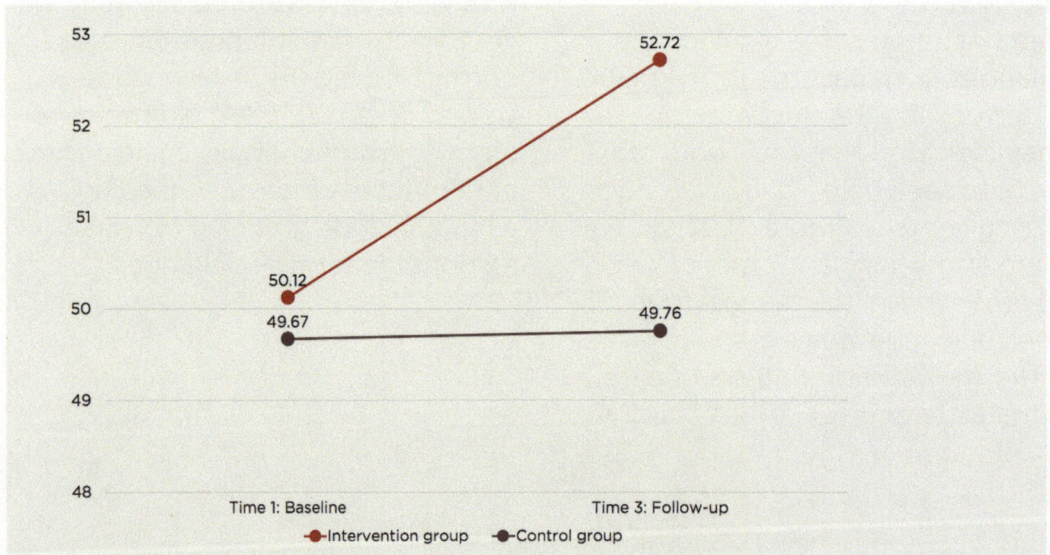

*Response to 10 General Help Seeking Questionnaire (GHSQ) questions
"How likely is it that you would recommend a male friend seek help from the
following people or services (e.g., intimate partner, friend, doctor)?" 10 questions
each scored from 1 (extremely unlikely) to 7 (extremely likely). Total score used
for analysis; means for each group reported here.

Figure 4: Change in help-seeking intentions – female friend*

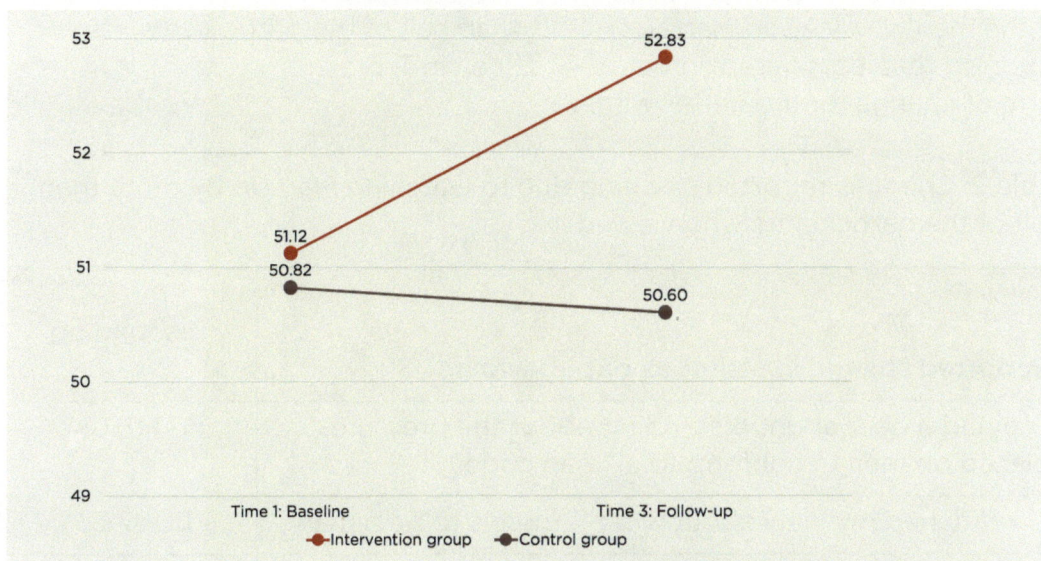

*Response to 10 General Help Seeking Questionnaire (GHSQ) questions "How likely is it that you would recommend a female friend seek help from the following people or services (e.g., intimate partner, friend, doctor)?" 10 questions each scored from 1 (extremely unlikely) to 7 (extremely likely). Total score used for analysis; means for each group reported here.

Figure 5: Change in conformity to masculine norms*

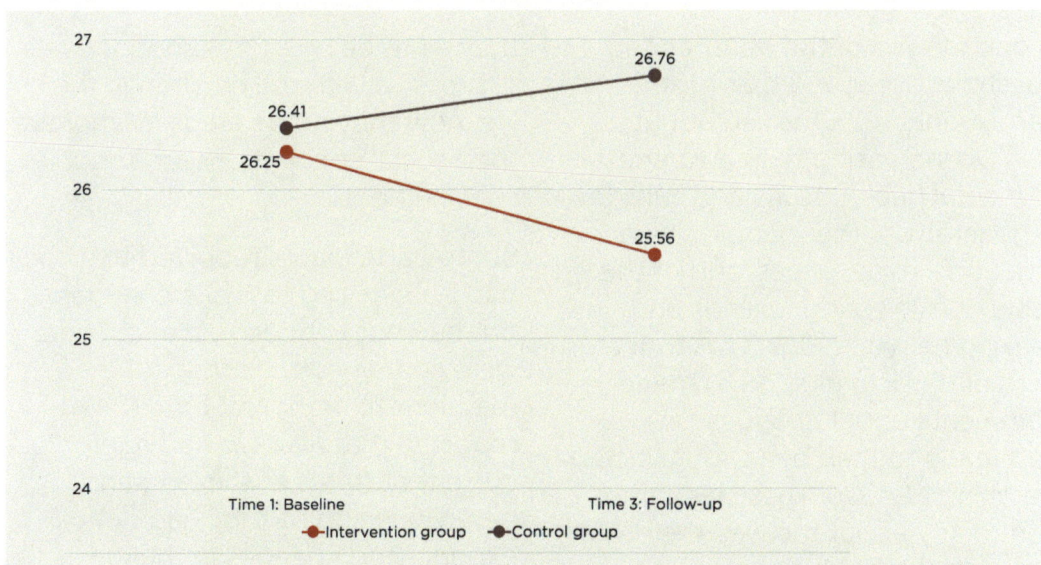

*Response to 22 Conformity to Masculine Norms Inventory (CMNI) questions e.g., "I like to talk about my feelings?" 22 questions scored from 0 (strongly disagree) to 3 (strongly agree). Total score used for analysis; means for each group reported here.

In the four-week follow-up to viewing the documentary, 142 (84%) of the men who viewed *Man Up* reported that it triggered some form of change for the better within them. The most commonly reported changes (each endorsed by more than half of the participants) can be seen in Table 2.

Table 2: Changes reported as being due to watching *Man Up* by more than half of the participants who viewed it

Reported change in attitudes or behaviours	Freq (%) responding "Yes"
I gained a deeper understanding about the pressures placed on men to conform to a "man code"	131 (87.3)
I broadened my view about what it means to be a man	110 (73.3)
I became more confident about reaching out to someone who I know is struggling	105 (70.0)
I changed my behaviours or attitudes based on my new understanding of the "man code"	95 (63.3)
I offered a friend time to talk	91 (60.7)
I looked after my health better	83 (55.3)

In our analysis of the open-ended questions, we found that most participants (82%) talked about *Man Up* increasing their awareness of mental health issues and suicide in general, of other people's inner emotional experiences, and of the value of expressing feelings and seeking help (see Box 3). About a third of participants (38%) made comments about changes they had made to their behaviour since watching *Man Up*. These were most commonly about the way they supported others, or about how they expressed their feelings or concerns (see Box 4). Less commonly participants commented on the way they were being more emotional expressive with the children in their life, how they made steps to improve their social connections, or about seeking help.

Some participants reported that they had been trying to make changes, but had not yet been able to. There were some neutral or negative reactions to *Man Up*. Some (24%) reported that *Man Up* had reinforced current patterns of thinking and behaviour, and so they had not experienced changes in their lives as a result of viewing the documentary.

Box 3: Increases in awareness that participants attributed to watching *Man Up*

"I did not realise the prevalence of male depression and suicide across the social spectrum."

"It brought to the forefront of my attention how everyone is fighting a battle and as mentioned before, wanting people to know they can come and talk to me about anything."

"I liked the line that went something like: 'If your car was bogged you would call your mate first thing no worries but if it's something affecting your own mental health you won't'. Kind of just highlights that we're willing to ask our mates for help, but for something as important as mental health we still struggle to reach out."

Box 4: Positive changes in behaviour that participants attributed to watching *Man Up*

"It made me reach out to my brother who is going through a difficult relationship breakdown and make sure he knows I'm here for him."

"I have noticed that when talking to other males I now pay more attention to what they are saying and how they are saying it, and have asked if they are ok more often."

THE ONLINE SURVEY

We conducted a repeat cross-sectional survey, making a version of the survey available on the *Man Up* website before the documentary was screened, and modifying it slightly after the documentary went to air. The two versions of the survey were promoted through various channels.

Both versions of the survey included three questions related to the changes that we hoped *Man Up* would contribute to: "If you were having personal or emotional problems, how likely would you be to ask for help from someone you know, or from a healthcare service?", "As a man, do you feel pressure from society to keep your feelings to yourself/appear strong all the time?", and "Would you like to have a closer relationship with your male friends?". The post-screening version of the survey contained additional questions about whether respondents had viewed *Man Up*, and, if so, whether they would recommend it to friends or family, and whether it changed the way they thought about the term "man up". It also asked about the likelihood that they would do anything different as a result of watching the documentary, such as spending more time with their male friends. The post-screening version also included opportunities for free-text comments.

THE RESULTS

In total, 1,287 respondents completed the survey. 476 completed the pre-screening survey (Group A); 192 completed the post-screening survey and had not viewed *Man Up* (Group B); and 619 completed the post-screening survey and had viewed *Man Up* (Group C; see Box 5).

Box 5: Groups responding to pre- and post-screening surveys

Respondents	Total	1,287
Pre-Screening	GROUP A	476
SCREENING		
Post-Screening HAD NOT viewed	GROUP B	192
Post-Screening HAD viewed	GROUP C	619

We argued that Group A represented men in a world before *Man Up*. We hypothesised that those in Group B would be no different to those in Group A in terms of their responses to the survey's key questions, because they had not been exposed to *Man Up*'s messages. By contrast, we hypothesised that because they had viewed *Man Up* those in Group C would be significantly more likely than those in Group A to ask for help, recognise pressures from society to hide their feelings and appear strong, and desire closer relationships with their male friends.

We found support for our first set of hypotheses: those in Group B were no different to those in Group A. We found support for two of the hypotheses in our second set. Compared with those in Group A, those in Group C were more likely to acknowledge societal pressures to repress their emotions and be stoic (AOR = 1.71, 95%CI = 1.07-2.75), and to express a wish for closer relationships with their male friends (AOR = 2.17, 95%CI = 1.39-3.40). We interpreted this as evidence that *Man Up* had successfully raised awareness of the power that society exerts over the way men feel and act, and that its messages about "mates supporting mates" had been well received.

We were surprised to find that there was no difference between those in Group C and those in Group A in terms of their likelihood of seeking help if they were having personal or emotional problems, given that we had found that viewing *Man Up* was associated with an increased likelihood of help-seeking in our RCT. We note, however, that our survey respondents exhibited a generally high level of openness to help-seeking, irrespective of which group they were in. This may reflect a selection bias, where men who were relatively more inclined to seek help might also have been more likely to complete the survey, regardless of whether they had viewed *Man Up* or not.

We delved more deeply into the responses of Group C, examining their reactions to *Man Up*. Overall, there were positive responses to the show. Almost all (98%) indicated that they would recommend it to others, and about two-thirds (64%) said that it changed the way they thought about the term "man up". We also found that they were highly likely to undertake a range of positive actions (e.g., offering a friend time to talk) as indicated by their responses to a series of specific prompts (see Table 3) and by their free-text comments (see Box 6).

Table 3: Likelihood of undertaking actions as a result of watching *Man Up*

As a result of watching the documentary, how likely are you to:	Mean rating*
Offer a friend time to talk?	4.2
Encourage a friend to seek help?	4.2
Raise awareness about male suicide in Australia, through actions or conversations?	4.2
Broaden your view about what it means to be a man?	3.9
Look after your health better?	3.9
Spend more time with your male friends?	3.6
Open up to someone about an issue you've been keeping to yourself?	3.6
Take conversations with your male friends to a deeper level?	3.6
Talk to friends and family about what it means to be a man?	3.5
See a health professional for advice?	3.5
Invest time in making new friends?	3.4

*Rated on a scale of 1 ("extremely unlikely") to 5 ("extremely likely")

Box 6: Positive responses to *Man Up*

"... The biggest thing I got from the program is wanting to be more open with my kids as they grow older and help break society's perception through them. Also I want to encourage them to show their feelings and I want to be available to their emotions. Thank you."

"The series came along at the right time for me. I suffer from anxiety and depression. Although I've never being suicidal I have had a couple of breakdowns in the last few months. I'd already decided to take ownership of my illness and seek help and reached out to a family member. The show made it easier for conversations to start..."

"This has been one of the most inspiring pieces of television I have ever seen. I honestly cannot thank everyone involved enough for what you have done, and are doing, to change the stigma around men's mental health [...] I am so inspired by these documentaries that I want to get more involved with these types of initiatives to share my story. To let men know it's okay to not be okay. That it's ok to ask for help. I've now learnt that showing vulnerability and emotion is far more courageous than holding it in. Letting it out is true strength. And that is what a real man is. Thank you Gus."

"Thank you ABC. Thank you Movember. And thank you to all those that made this a brilliantly eye-opening documentary. You should all be so proud."

"... my wife and I both gained a great value from watching the documentary. She was once again exposed to those times of my downs and thoughts of suicide. It was great to have the opportunity to watch it together. Gus thank you for your efforts in putting this together. Let's hope that we can all make a change to the perception of MENtal health."

"Thank you. I'm a 16 year old male. I had one good mate this year became hospitalised for over two months due to suicidal actions and thoughts. I knew he was doing it rough but not that rough... I watched your video tonight about the talk at Gus's son's school and it made me realise how little I did for my mate, and how much of a role I also played in his condition ... I just want to thank you for opening my mind up about the unspoken issue of suicide for Australian men. I hope to do something about it myself in the near future. Thanks."

ANALYSES OF WEBSITE AND SOCIAL MEDIA DATA

There is increasing recognition that social media may have potential for suicide prevention, and may be particularly useful for reaching groups that are otherwise hard to reach, including men.[22,23] To our knowledge there are no precedents for the way in which we implemented the digital strategy alongside the television documentary's release, and so we felt that it was important to conduct analyses of website and social media data to examine the collective impact of the documentary and broader digital campaign.

We conducted an initial formative evaluation of the *Man Up* website and associated digital materials when we were developing them. We tested them through interviews with 17 men of different ages and diverse backgrounds with the intention of maximising their potential impact on help-seeking and challenging of masculine norms. From this process, four key themes emerged. Firstly, our participants highlighted that images used needed to be representative and relatable. Secondly, they had mixed views about the subject area of masculinity, with some indicating that the term "man up" made them keen to find out more about the documentary, and others expressing concern that it might turn men away from viewing the show. Thirdly, engaging with content about mental health difficulties and suicide was seen by some as a risk to their own reputations or to their relationships with others. Finally, participants tended to prefer active, direct communication that made it easier to understand the messages. These learnings helped shape the final website and associated materials.

Our main evaluation efforts in this area examined website, Twitter and Facebook activity during the 14-week digital campaign (15 August - 20 November 2016). We used Google Analytics to evaluate website performance in terms of attracting and engaging users during the digital campaign. Website engagement was measured by user behaviour on the site that included bounce rates (the percentage of sessions where the

#MANUP was the main hashtag used to promote the campaign. We also used #ABCMANUP, #LISTENUP and #SPEAKUP.

The official Facebook page is www.facebook.com/ManUpTVSeries

user looked only at that page), page views; pages per session, session duration, and sharing. We also used Google analytics to analyse help-seeking activity on the website, and completed a qualitative analysis of emails to the *Man Up* team that were sent through the website.

We collected Twitter data from two sources, one via the social media tool Twitter Insights, and the other through harvesting original content tweets using the free-of-charge Twitter Application Programming Interface (API). Using Twitter Insights we looked at reactions (retweets, replies, likes, profile clicks, URL clicks, hashtag clicks, expanded click, follows, views) to tweets posted by manuptvseries. We harvested original content to capture activity using the hashtag #MANUP in the 14 weeks

before the campaign, the 14 weeks during the campaign, and the 14 weeks after the campaign. We also conducted a qualitative analysis of tweets.

We also collected Facebook data from two sources. We downloaded data from the Facebook Insights to determine the overall reach of and reactions (responses, shares and comments) to the Facebook posts during the 14-week campaign period. We used the NCapture plug-in for Windows Explorer to downloaded Facebook content data, including initial posts and comments related to these posts, for the duration of the campaign. Again, we undertook a qualitative analysis to identify themes in the Facebook data.

THE RESULTS

In total, 54,969 *Man Up* website sessions were recorded from 43,140 users who made 103,243 page views (81,663 by new users, 21,580 by returning users) during the period of data collection. In total, there were 1,470 shares from the website indicating endorsement by users of website content. Of these 922 were shared to Facebook, 344 via email, and 204 to Twitter.

The website home page, "About" page and pages related to each of the episodes which featured a trailer, synopsis, photos and additional video extras were most commonly viewed. The pages related to each of the three episodes yielded the highest average times spent on page, which is probably due to people taking time to view the trailers on these pages.

The "Help a Mate" page was well utilised. It garnered 1,796 total page views, 1,587 of which were unique. There were 271 clicks on the links to listed support organisations, and an additional 36 clicks on links to organisations provided elsewhere on the website (307 in total). The most commonly clicked link was for the male-focused helpline service, MensLine Australia. There were 1,248 downloads of information from the website from various pages, including information about *Man Up* (446 downloads). Of the psychosocial resources, the three most frequently downloaded were "Men's experiences with suicidal behaviour and depression", "Men's help-seeking behaviour", and "Men's social connectedness" (428, 225, and 149 downloads respectively).

Over its whole duration, the *Man Up* social media campaign earned nearly 5,000 Twitter likes and 2,500 retweets and gained around 1,022,000 impressions (delivery of a post or tweet to an account's Twitter stream). 271 posts were published on the *Man Up* TV series Facebook wall (manuptvseries). These wall posts received 4,349 comments, ranging from one comment to up to 1,258 comments for a post during the campaign period.[a]

On average, Facebook posts and tweets that included a video prompted the highest number of likes and comments. By far the most successful Facebook post, with over 124,000 reactions, was about the release of the *Man Up, Speak Up* campaign ad that Gus created as part of Episode 3 (see Box 7). Similarly, the most successful tweet based on "reactions" was one that heralded the final episode before it went to air and provided a preview of the campaign ad (4,264 reactions).

(a) We restricted our qualitative analyses of tweets and Facebook comments to those that were directly triggered by *Man Up*. In the case of Twitter, we focused on a subset of 1,876 campaign-related tweets that included the hashtag #MANUP and at least one other hashtag that had been used at least 10 times during the campaign by manuptvseries, because #MANUP has other associations. In the case of Facebook, we used the 150 posts by *Man Up* (118) and external organisations (32) as our starting point and then examined the 4,053 comments associated with them.

We identified a number of core themes in our Twitter analysis: expressing emotions; mental health and suicide; men's issues (with sub-themes of being a man and fathering or raising boys); help-seeking; personal stories; and supporting others. Similar themes emerged when we examined the Facebook comments: expressing emotions; personal stories; masculinity; suicide; help seeking; and supporting others.

In both cases, the theme of expressing emotions was particularly prominent. So too was the theme of personal stories – many Twitter and Facebook users shared stories about growing up with pressure to "behave like a man", about important people in their lives, and about their experience of having lost someone to suicide. Similar themes were found in emails sent via the website (see Box 8).

> **Box 8: Examples of comments generated by the digital media campaign**
>
> *"Men need to learn to be more comfortable and able to sit with another man's distress. From what I see, their discomfort when a man shows distress causes them to pull back and shun that person, sometimes even cut the connection. This only adds to the distress and isolation. Society, the way men are socialised from birth and blokey culture have messed with men's capacity for compassion for each other. It stinks."* (Facebook comment)
>
> *"Just wanted to tell you how much I enjoyed watching your show on the ABC this last few weeks. I'm a 52 year old bloke with depression which is managed with medication but has still threatened to end relationships a few times. I really enjoyed your visit to your son's school and the honesty and courage shown by your son and his fellow students. It was bloody tear jerkingly fantastic."* (Email sent via website)
>
> *"I used the content to talk to the offenders in my group in maximum security. As I finished my talk to these vulnerable men, there was a knock at the door to advise one offender his little brother had committed suicide. It was devastating. Thanks for enabling me to talk with men."* (Email sent via website)

Collectively, the website, Twitter and Facebook data painted an overwhelmingly positive picture of the response to *Man Up*. We made just two observations that might temper these findings. The first is that when we looked at the gender of those who had posted comments on Facebook (the only platform for which we were able to do this analysis), we found that almost three quarters of the 2,290 comments were from females (arguably suggesting that males might still be less engaged with talking about suicide, expressing emotions and masculinity).

The second is that we did identify a very small number of negative comments (seven emails to the website with negative feedback, four negative tweets, and 30 negative comments posted to Facebook).

All but two of the negative Facebook comments were from men; several rejected the idea that men should openly express their feelings – for example, *"Unfortunately when they do talk, reach out for help or make themselves vulnerable, they are mocked for it, so it is often a no-win situation."* Another group of

Facebook comments made a link between male suicide and unfair treatment of men in the Family Court; some argued that feminism is to blame for higher male suicide rates. There were some comments to Facebook and in emails about the lack of diversity in ethnicity and sexuality in *Man Up*, and the lack of attention to the role of women.

We concluded from the above analyses that the *Man Up* digital media campaign triggered conversations about masculinity and suicide that might otherwise not have happened – both online, and in people's lives. For some this may have prompted a shift towards expressing emotions and reaching out to others for help. The campaign was particularly effective in disseminating information and promoting conversations in real-time, an advantage that it had over more traditional health promotion campaigns. There was considerable evidence of help-seeking by website users. There are several lessons about increasing the effectiveness of a digital media strategy, including the value of certain kinds of content (particularly videos), and increasing the information available from the website. Light-hearted website content worked well to direct users to help-seeking.

COMBINATION DATA SOURCES

As noted above, we conducted two additional evaluation exercises that drew on several of the above data sources simultaneously. The first of these was an analysis of the free-text responses to a specific question that we asked of participants in the RCT and respondents to the online survey: "Did watching the documentary change the way you view the term 'man up'? If so, how?"

The second exercise drew on free-text responses made by RCT participants, as well as quantitative and qualitative data from the analyses of website and social media activity. We analysed all of these to identify instances where people had commented on particular segments of the documentary that resonated with them. We did this with a view to determining which were the key ingredients of the success of *Man Up*.

THE RESULTS

In total, 307 men provided feedback on the question about the way watching *Man Up* changed the way they viewed the term "man up" (96 RCT participants and 210 online survey respondents). Most of these men indicated that the documentary had caused them to re-think stereotypes of masculinity, and consider a greater diversity of attitudes and behaviours as relevant to "being a man". Many commented that they now interpreted "man up" as a call for men to be open about their emotions and connect with others. We interpreted this as further evidence of *Man Up* having a positive impact on men's views of masculinity.

There were two stand-out segments in the show. The first related to a workshop with teenage boys at the high school attended by Gus Worland's son Jack, led by facilitator Tom Harkin. The workshop explored the pressures of masculinity on the boys and triggered some extraordinarily raw and open discussion, that was listened to by all present with complete respect. The workshop segment itself appeared in Episode 2, but it was also referenced at other points through the documentary (e.g., there was also an informal discussion between Gus and the school boys about expressing emotions and crying). This content was by far the best received of participants in the randomised controlled trial (117 positive comments immediately post viewing, 89 at four-week follow-up). A large number of Facebook comments highlighted the importance of this workshop and suggested it should be available to all schools. The "Boys to Men" website page, which includes information on the initiative in schools, had the highest bounce rate of any page, indicating that many users came directly to the site to view only that page. Ninety-five tweets directly referred to this workshop, including many positive responses by followers (see Box 9).

Box 9: Example responses to the segment showing the workshop with the boys at Gus's son's school (and related segments)

"The biggest impact was the workshop for the year 10 boys. Watching them transform from bravado to respectful was totally mind blowing." (Comment from RCT participant)

"#manup is the best show on TV right now. That high school workshop - should be compulsory in schools. Brilliant." (Twitter post)

The second stand-out segment was the one in which Gus created his *Man Up, Speak Up* campaign ad and screened it to selected men whom he had met on his journey. This segment appeared in Episode 3. It was the second most popular segment for participants in the randomised controlled trial (50 positive comments immediately post viewing, 12 at four-week follow up). It attracted the greatest number of comments on Twitter, being mentioned in 224 tweets or retweets that promoted the campaign, encouraged others to watch it, or were positive in other ways (see Box 10). At the end of the digital campaign, the ad had had over 40 million views;[24] we believe that this figure is now closer to 50 million.

Another popular segment was one showing Gus making a behind-the-scenes visit to Lifeline in which viewers could hear Lifeline telephone counsellors respond to a range of calls; one male counsellor was involved in a particularly moving call with someone who was clearly on the brink of self-harm. Audiences also responded well to segments involving personal accounts from people who had made a suicide attempt or been bereaved by suicide, particularly those in rural areas. Many people expressed interest in the information about male suicide in Australia that was presented across all three episodes, mainly through interviews with expert interviews and discussion of statistics.

There were however some comments that *Man Up* lacked diversity. For example, one participant in the RCT made the following comment: *"Generally very white. Not representative of other non-white Australian males. Not much in terms of gender and sexual identity."*

Why do we tell boys to stop crying?

Man up. Speak up.

5. CONCLUSION

One of the stand-out risk factors for poor mental health and well-being and heightened levels of suicidality in men is conformity to traditional masculine norms, particularly those that deter men from reaching out when they need help.

Our RCT showed that *Man Up* was efficacious in terms of increasing men's likelihood of seeking help in tough times and encouraging their friends to do the same, and shifting their views of masculinity. Our online survey suggested that it was effective in enabling men to recognise societal pressures to repress their emotions and be stoic, and increasing their desires for closer relationships with their male friends. These impacts were further underscored by the wealth of positive emails and social media posts about changes in men's attitudes and behaviours. These outcomes are positive and are made all the more so by the fact that the documentary, and the digital campaign that surrounded it, had such a broad reach.

The analyses of *Man Up*'s components point to the value of using media-based interventions to bring about positive change, particularly for groups which may be hard to reach by other means. We have also identified a number of lessons about what appeals to audiences and what messages and approaches resonate. These have applicability to others seeking innovative solutions to men's mental health and help seeking behaviour.

More immediately, our evaluation suggests that the visibility of *Man Up* itself should be maintained and built upon. Opportunities for screening *Man Up* in different contexts and for different audiences should be explored, both within Australia and overseas. Broadening the reach of *Man Up*'s messages has the potential to save the lives of men around the world by shining a spotlight on the relationship between masculinity and suicide.

REFERENCES

1. Australian Bureau of Statistics (ABS). Causes of Death, Australia, 2016. Canberra: ABS, 2017.

2. Pirkis J, Spittal M, Keogh L, Mousaferiadis T, Currier D. Masculinity and suicidal thinking. Social Psychiatry and Psychiatric Epidemiology 2016; 52(3): 319-27.

3. Boman E, Walker G. Predictors of men's health care utlization. Psychology of Men and Masculinity 2010; 11(2): 113-22.

4. Coleman D. Traditional masculinity as a risk factor for suicidal ideation: Cross-sectional and prospective evidence from a study of young adults. Archives of Suicide Research 2015; 19(3): 366-84.

5. Rice S, Fallon B, Bambling M. Men and depression: The impact of masculine role norms throughout the lifespan. The Educational and Developmental Psychologist 2011; 28(2): 133-44.

6. Thompson E, Pleck J. Masculinity ideologies: A review of research instrumentation on men and masculinities. In: Levant R, Pollack W, eds. A New Psychology of Men. New York: Basic Books; 1995.

7. Wong Y, Ho M-H, S-Y. W, Miller I. Meta-analyses of the relationship between conformity to masculine norms and mental health-related outcomes. Journal of Counseling Psychology 2017; 64(1): 80-93.

8. Galdas P, Cheater F, Marshall P. Men and health help-seeking behaviour: Literature review. Journal of Advanced Nursing 2005; 49(6): 616-23.

9. Nam S, Chu H, Lee M, Lee J, Kim N, Lee S. A meta-analysis of gender differences in attitudes toward seeking professional psychological help. Journal of American College Health 2010; 59(2): 110-6.

10. Mahalik J, Locke B, Ludlow L, et al. Development of the Conformity to Masculine Norms Inventory. Psychology of Men and Masculinity 2003; 4(1): 3-25.

11. Vogel D, Heimerdinger-Edwards S, Hammer J, Hubbard A. 'Boys don't cry': Examination of the links between endorsement of masculine norms, self-stigma, and help-seeking attitudes for men from diverse backgrounds. Journal of Counseling Psychology 2011; 58(3): 368-82.

12. Vogel D, Wester S, Hammer J, Downing-Matibag T. Referring men to seek help: The influence of gender role conflict and stigma. Psychology of Men and Masculinity 2014; 15(1): 60-7.

13. King K, Schlichthorst M, Spittal M, Phelps A, Pirkis J. Can a documentary increase help-seeking intentions in men? A randomised controlled trial. Journal of Epidemiology and Community Health 2017: DOI: 10.1136/jech-2017-209502.

14. King K, Schlichthorst M, Reifels L, et al. Impacts of a documentary about masculinity and men's health. Submitted.

15. Schlichthorst M, King K, Spittal M, Reifels L, Phelps A, Pirkis J. Using a television documentary to prevent suicide in men and boys. Australasian Psychiatry 2018: DOI: 10.1177/1039856217749022.

16. King K, Schlichthorst M, Turnure J, Phelps A, Pirkis J. Using Google analytics to explore the effectiveness of television documentary website to promote help-seeking. In preparation.

17. Schlichthorst M, King K, Reifels L, Phelps A, Pirkis J. Using a television documentary to prompt conversations on male suicide, masculinity and help-seeking: An evaluation of Facebook data. In preparation.

18. Schlichthorst M, King K, Turnure J, Phelps A, Pirkis J. Communicating with men about masculinity and suicide: Testing social media materials and a website for a television documentary. In preparation.

19. Schlichthorst M, King K, Turnure J, Sukunesan S, Phelps A, Pirkis J. Influencing the conversation about masculinity and suicide: Using Twitter data in the evaluation of the *"Man Up"* multi- media campaign. Journal of Medical Internet Research 2018; 5(1): e14.

20. Schlichthorst M, King K, Phelps A, Pirkis J. *Man Up* – multimedia intervention to tackle male suicide: What worked? In preparation.

21. Wilson C, Deane F, Ciarrochi J, Rickwood D. Measuring help-seeking intentions: Properties of the general help-seeking questionnaire. Canadian Journal of Counselling 2005; 39(15-28).

22. Clarke J, Van Amerom G. A comparison of blogs by depressed men and women. Issues in Mental Health Nursing 2008; 29(3): 243-64.

23. Luxton D, June J, Fairall J. Social media and suicide: a public health perspective. American Journal of Public Health 2012; 102(S2): S195-S200.

24. Turnure J. *Man Up* Digital Campaign Wrap Report. Sydney: Heiress Films, 2017.

www.ingramcontent.com/pod-product-compliance
Lightning Source LLC
Chambersburg PA
CBHW040932050426
42334CB00049B/65